States

NEBRASKA

by Jordan Mills

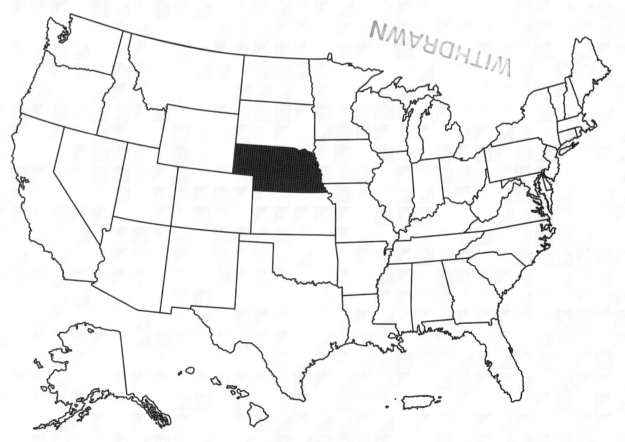

CAPSTONE PRESS
a capstone imprint

Next Page Books are published by Capstone Press,
1710 Roe Crest Drive, North Mankato, Minnesota 56003
www.mycapstone.com

Library of Congress Cataloging-in-Publication Data
Cataloging-in-publication information is on file with the Library of
Congress.
ISBN 978-1-5157-0414-0 (library binding)
ISBN 978-1-5157-0473-7 (paperback)
ISBN 978-1-5157-0525-3 (ebook PDF)

Editorial Credits
Jaclyn Jaycox, editor; Richard Korab and Katy LaVigne, designers;
Morgan Walters, media researcher; Tori Abraham, production specialist

Photo Credits
Capstone Press: Angi Gahler, map 4, 7; CriaImages.com: Jay Robert
Nash Collection, middle 19, top left 21; Dreamstime: Fotoeye75, 10;
Getty Images: MPI/Stringer, 25; Library of Congress: Prints and
Photographs Division, bottom 19, Carl Van Vechten, bottom 18, George
Grantham Bain Collection, middle 18, New York World-Telegram and
the Sun Newspaper Photograph Collection/Ed Ford, top 18, 27, William
Charles Thompson, Alhambra, California, top 19; Newscom: Andre
Jenny Stock Connection Worldwide, 26, Chuck Haney/DanitaDelimont.
com "Danita Delimont Photography," 7, Credit GENE BLEVINS/
REUTERS, 29, Everett Collection, 28; North Wind Picture Archives, 12;
One Mile Up, Inc., flag, seal 23; Shutterstock: aimy27feb, top 24, Alf
Ribeiro, 15, Cartela, top left 20, Daniel Prudek, bottom left 21, Dave
Weaver, 6, 16, Elena Elisseeva, top right 20, George Burba, bottom
right 8, Katherine Welles, 13, Melanie Metz, bottom left 8, Oxana
Denezhkina, bottom 24, Potapov Alexander, middle left 21, rthoma, 17,
Sergey Goruppa, bottom right 20, Sharon Day, cover, Suzanne Tucker,
5, Tom Middleton, 14, Tom Reichner, bottom left 20, middle right 21,
Warren Price Photography, bottom right 21, Zack Frank, 11; United
States Department of Agriculture/Lynn Betts, top right 21; Wikimedia:
Bkell, 9

All design elements by Shutterstock

Printed and bound in China.
0316/CA21600187
012016 009436F16

TABLE OF CONTENTS

Want to take your research further? Ask your librarian if your school subscribes to PebbleGo Next. If so, when you see this helpful symbol 🔺 throughout the book, log onto www.pebblegonext.com for bonus downloads and information.

LOCATION

Nebraska is one of the upper plains states. South Dakota lies to the north. The Missouri River flows for 450 miles (724 kilometers) along Nebraska's eastern border, separating it from Iowa and Missouri. Kansas and Colorado lie to the south. Wyoming is located to the west. Lincoln is the capital of Nebraska. The state's largest cities are Lincoln, Omaha, Bellevue, and Grand Island.

PebbleGo Next Bonus!
To print and label your own map, go to www.pebblegonext.com and search keywords:
NE MAP

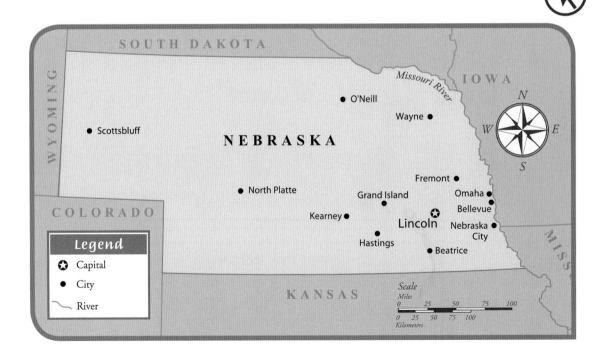

Omaha is Nebraska's largest city and is located on the west bank of the Missouri River.

GEOGRAPHY

The Great Plains area covers most of Nebraska. The Sand Hills region is in northern Nebraska. It is the largest area of sand dunes in North America. The High Plains and the Loess Plains make up the rest of the Great Plains in Nebraska.

Nebraska has more miles of rivers than any other state. The main river in Nebraska is the Platte River. The state's highest point, Panorama Point, is in western Nebraska. It is 5,426 feet (1,654 meters) tall.

PebbleGo Next Bonus!
To watch a video about
Homestead National
Monument, go to
www.pebblegonext.com
and search keywords:
NE VIDEO

A powerful storm tore through Valentine in July 2005, causing extensive damage. The following year, a wildfire nearly destroyed the town.

A scenic overlook in Niobrara State Park offers a view of the Missouri River in northern Nebraska.

High Plains

Sand Hills

GREAT PLAINS

Missouri River

Loess Hills

North Platte River

DISSECTED TILL PLAINS

Panorama Point

Lake McConaughy

South Platte River

Loess Plains

Platte River

Legend

▲ Highest Point

Lake

River

Sand Hills

Scale

Miles
0   25   50   75   100

0   25   50   75   100
Kilometers

WEATHER

Nebraska's weather changes often. Rainfall amounts change, bringing flooding one year and drought the next. The average January temperature is 23 degrees Fahrenheit (minus 5 degrees Celsius). The average July temperature is 76°F (24°C).

Average High and Low Temperatures (Lincoln, NE)

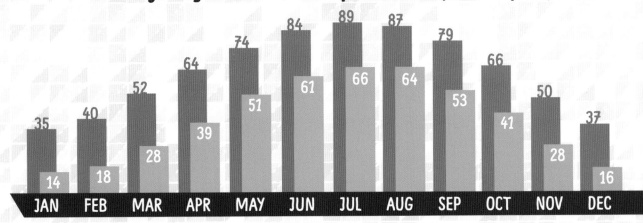

	JAN	FEB	MAR	APR	MAY	JUN	JUL	AUG	SEP	OCT	NOV	DEC
High	35	40	52	64	74	84	89	87	79	66	50	37
Low	14	18	28	39	51	61	66	64	53	41	28	16

LANDMARKS

Nebraska National Forest

The Nebraska National Forest includes the world's largest hand-planted forest. Its ponderosa pine trees cover about 25,000 acres (10,117 hectares) of land.

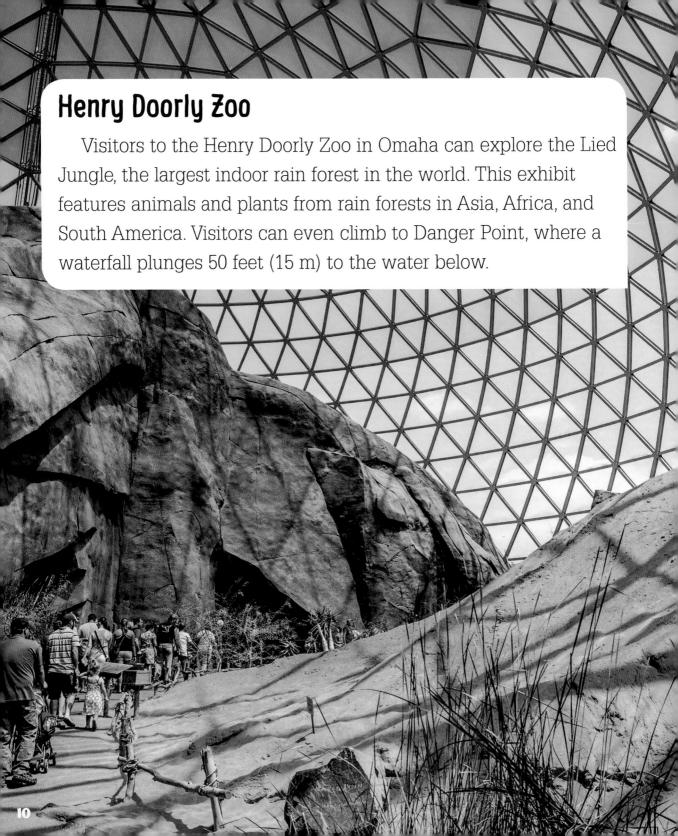

Henry Doorly Zoo

Visitors to the Henry Doorly Zoo in Omaha can explore the Lied Jungle, the largest indoor rain forest in the world. This exhibit features animals and plants from rain forests in Asia, Africa, and South America. Visitors can even climb to Danger Point, where a waterfall plunges 50 feet (15 m) to the water below.

Chimney Rock

Chimney Rock is a famous natural rock formation near the North Platte River in western Nebraska. It was a major landmark for pioneer travelers on the Oregon Trail. The formation's tip is 325 feet (99 m) above the base.

HISTORY AND GOVERNMENT

Hundreds of settlers passed through Nebraska on the Oregon Trail during the Great Migration.

Many American Indians once lived in Nebraska. In 1541 Francisco Vásquez de Coronado claimed southwestern North America for Spain. In 1682 French explorer René-Robert Cavelier, known as Sieur de La Salle, claimed parts of present-day Nebraska for France. Control of the area changed often. Then in 1803 the United States purchased the Louisiana Territory, which included present-day Nebraska.

Pioneers began crossing Nebraska on the Oregon Trail in 1843. Congress established Kansas Territory and Nebraska Territory in 1854. New settlers poured in. The Homestead Act of 1862 attracted more newcomers. In 1867 Nebraska became the 37th U.S. state.

Nebraska's government has three branches. The governor leads the executive branch. Nebraska's legislature, which creates laws, has 49 members. Nebraska is the only state that has a one-house legislature. The state's judicial branch, which includes the courts, upholds the laws.

Two state capitol buildings preceded the current building located in Lincoln.

INDUSTRY

Agriculture is the biggest business in Nebraska. Livestock is the state's largest agricultural industry. Nearly 50 percent of all agriculture income in Nebraska comes from livestock sales. Cattle provide the most farm income. Hogs, sheep, and poultry make up the rest. Corn is Nebraska's leading crop. Other top crops in Nebraska are beans, soybeans, wheat, hay, and sugar beets.

Food processing is a big part of Nebraska's economy too. Many Nebraska companies pack beef, pork, and poultry. Other companies process corn products, canned and frozen fruits and vegetables, and potato chips.

Cattle outnumber people in Nebraska by about four to one.

Nebraska has a variety of other manufacturing companies. Some factories make dog and cat food, paint, cleaning supplies, or plastic bags. Other plants make farm machinery, irrigation systems, and electrical equipment.

Plants in Omaha manufacture farm equipment, the state's most important kind of machinery.

POPULATION

Most people in Nebraska have European heritage. Their families traveled to the state from Czechoslovakia, Italy, Germany, Sweden, Denmark, Ireland, Spain, and other European countries. Today more than 1.4 million Nebraskans are white. Hispanics are the state's second-largest ethnic group. About 167,000 Hispanics live in Nebraska. About 80,000 residents are African-American. More than 30,000 Asians live in Nebraska.

Population by Ethnicity

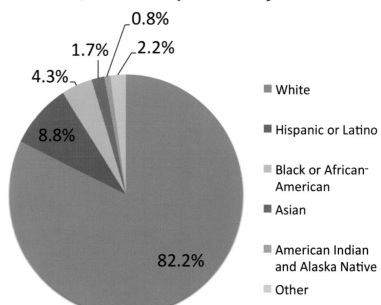

- White
- Hispanic or Latino
- Black or African-American
- Asian
- American Indian and Alaska Native
- Other

Source: U.S. Census Bureau.

FAMOUS PEOPLE

Malcolm X (1925–1965) was a civil rights leader. He was born Malcolm Little in Omaha.

Grover Cleveland Alexander (1887–1950) was one of the greatest pitchers in baseball history. He played with the Philadelphia Phillies and the Chicago Cubs. He was born in Elba.

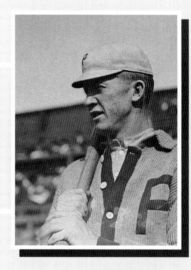

Willa Cather (1875–1947) was an author who wrote *O Pioneers!* (1913) and many other novels. She was born in Virginia and grew up in Red Cloud.

Standing Bear (1829–1908) was a Ponca chief who fought for American Indians' rights to their land. He was born on a Ponca reservation in northeastern Nebraska.

Johnny Carson (1925–2005) was a comedian who hosted the late-night talk show *The Tonight Show* from 1962 to 1992. He was born in Iowa but grew up in Norfolk.

Gerald Ford (1913–2006) was the 38th president of the United States (1974–1977). He was born in Omaha. He grew up in Grand Rapids, Michigan.

STATE SYMBOLS

Tree

cottonwood

Flower

goldenrod

Bird

western meadowlark

Fish

channel catfish

PebbleGo Next Bonus! To make a dessert using Nebraska's state drink, go to www.pebblegonext.com and search keywords:
NE RECIPE

Fossil

mammoth

Grass

little bluestem

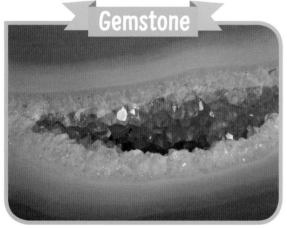

Gemstone

blue agate

Animal

white-tailed deer

Insect

honeybee

Soft Drink

Kool-Aid

FAST FACTS

STATEHOOD
1867

CAPITAL ☆
Lincoln

LARGEST CITY •
Omaha

SIZE
76,824 square miles (198,973 square kilometers) land area
(2010 U.S. Census Bureau)

POPULATION
1,868,516 (2013 U.S. Census estimate)

STATE NICKNAME
Cornhusker State

STATE MOTTO
"Equality before the law"

STATE SEAL

Nebraska's state seal shows a farmer with a hammer and anvil. Behind the farmer, a settler's cabin sits near sheaves of wheat and stalks of corn. A steamboat travels on the Missouri River. A train heads toward the Rocky Mountains. The state motto, "Equality before the law," is written on a banner at the top of the seal.

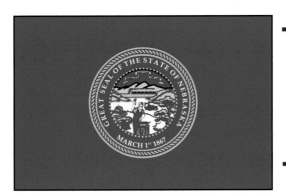

STATE FLAG

On Nebraska's flag, the state seal is printed in gold and silver. The seal shows a farmer with a hammer and anvil. A settler's cabin sits near sheaves of wheat and stalks of corn. A steamboat and a train are also featured. The state motto is written on a banner at the top of the seal. The flag's background is blue. The state adopted the flag in 1925. Until 1963 the flag was called a banner. That year lawmakers changed the name from banner to flag.

MINING PRODUCTS

petroleum, sand and gravel, lime, limestone, portland cement

MANUFACTURED GOODS

food products, chemicals, machinery, fabricated metal products, motor vehicle parts, plastics and rubber products, computer and electronic equipment, printed material

FARM PRODUCTS

beef, hogs, sheep, poultry, corn, soybeans, Great Northern beans, wheat, popcorn

PebbleGo Next Bonus! To learn the lyrics to the state song, go to www.pebblegonext.com and search keywords:

NE SONG

NEBRASKA TIMELINE

1541 Francisco Vásquez de Coronado claims southwestern North America for Spain. His group meets the Pawnee, Omaha, Ponca, and other American Indians.

1620 The Pilgrims establish a colony in the New World in present-day Massachusetts.

1682 René-Robert Cavelier, known as Sieur de La Salle, claims parts of present-day Nebraska for France.

1720 The Pawnee defeat Pedro de Villasur's Spanish army, which was trying to reclaim the Nebraska area.

1775–1783 American colonists and the British fight the Revolutionary War.

1803 The United States buys the Louisiana Territory, including Nebraska, from France. The sale is called the Louisiana Purchase.

1819 U.S. Army troops set up Fort Atkinson near present-day Omaha to protect the fur trade and keep peace with American Indians.

1843 Thousands of pioneers travel west to build farms and homes. This westward movement across Nebraska becomes known as the Great Migration.

1854 Congress passes the Kansas-Nebraska Act and creates the Nebraska Territory.

1861–1865 The Union and the Confederacy fight the Civil War. About 3,000 men from Nebraska Territory fight on the Union side.

1867 Nebraska becomes the 37th state on March 1.

1905 The North Platte River Project begins. It brings water to crops in western Nebraska.

1914–1918

World War I is fought; the United States enters the war in 1917.

1917

Father Edward J. Flanagan of Omaha opens Boys Town, a home for neglected boys from across the country.

1939–1945

World War II is fought; the United States enters the war in 1941.

1963

Nebraska begins to broadcast educational TV programming to the entire state.

1986 Kay Orr and Helen Boosalis run for governor. This race is the first time two women run for governor of any state.

1997 University of Nebraska Cornhuskers are national football champions for the fifth time.

2012 Four tornadoes strike near North Platte, damaging homes, derailing railroad cars, and injuring four people.

2015 Nebraska Medicine Transplant Center re-launches lung transplant program.

Glossary

anvil *(AN-vuhl)*—the flat-faced piece of metal on an ice hammer; climbers use the anvil to pound protective hardware into ice and rock

ethnic *(ETH-nik)*—related to a group of people and their culture

executive *(ig-ZE-kyuh-tiv)*—the branch of government that makes sure laws are followed

heritage *(HER-uh-tij)*—the culture and traditions of one's family, ancestors, or country

industry *(IN-duh-stree)*—a business which produces a product or provides a service

irrigation *(ihr-uh-GAY-shuhn)*—bringing water to dry soil through methods such as pipes and channels

judicial *(joo-DISH-uhl)*—to do with the branch of government that explains and interprets the laws

landmark *(LAND-mark)*—object that help identify a location

legislature *(LEJ-iss-lay-chur)*—a group of elected officials who have the power to make or change laws for a country or state

neglect *(ni-GLEKT)*—the failure to take care of or pay attention to something or someone

petroleum *(puh-TROH-lee-uhm)*—an oily liquid found below the earth's surface used to make gasoline, heating oil, and many other products

Read More

Bailer, Darice. *What's Great About Nebraska?* Our Great States. Minneapolis: Lerner Publications Company, 2015.

Ganeri, Anita. *United States of America: A Benjamin Blog and His Inquisitive Dog Guide.* Country Guides. Chicago: Heinemann Raintree, 2015.

Sanders, Doug. *Nebraska.* It's My State! New York: Cavendish Square Publishing, 2014.

Internet Sites

FactHound offers a safe, fun way to find Internet sites related to this book. All of the sites on FactHound have been researched by our staff.

Here's all you do:

Visit *www.facthound.com*

Type in this code: 9781515704140

 Check out projects, games and lots more at **www.capstonekids.com**

Critical Thinking Using the Common Core

1. Which states border Nebraska? Use the map on page 4 for help. (Key Ideas and Details)

2. What can you find at the Henry Doorly Zoo? (Key Ideas and Details)

3. An anvil is featured on Nebraska's state seal and state flag. What is an anvil? (Craft and Structure)

Index